The Civil War and Reconstruction

Rebellion and Rebuilding

Mr. Lincoln

Compiled by Joanne Randolph

PowerKiDS press

Published in 2018 by The Rosen Publishing Group, Inc.
29 East 21st Street, New York, NY 10010

From Cobblestone Magazine (May 1995):
"Trying Times: The Civil War President" by Harold Holzer
"The 'Great Emancipator'" by Harold Holzer
"'I Laugh, Because I Must Not Cry'" by Carolyn Liberatore Lavine
"Lincoln's Other Wartime Triumphs" by Harold Holzer

Cataloging-in-Publication Data

Names: Randolph, Joanne.
Title: Mr. Lincoln / compiled by Joanne Randolph.
Description: New York : PowerKids Press, 2018. | Series: The Civil War and Reconstruction: rebellion and rebuilding | Includes glossary and index.
Identifiers: LCCN ISBN 9781538340943 (pbk.) | ISBN 9781538340936 (library bound) | ISBN 9781538340950 (6 pack)
Subjects: LCSH: Lincoln, Abraham, 1809-1865--Juvenile literature. | Presidents--United States--Biography--Juvenile literature.
Classification: LCC E457.905 M578 2018 | DDC 973.7092 B--dc23

Designer: Katelyn E. Reynolds
Editor: Joanne Randolph

Photo credits: Cvr, p. 1 Oscar White/Corbis/VCG via Getty Images; cvr, pp. 1–32 (background texture) javarman/Shutterstock.com; cvr, pp. 1–32 (flags) cybrain/Shutterstock.com; cvr, pp. 1–32 (scroll) Seregam/Shutterstock.com; pp. 5, 6, 8, 12, 20, 23, 24, 29 courtesy of the Library of Congress; p. Brady National Photographic Art Gallery (Washington, D.C.) 1858- ?, Photographer/U.S. National Archives & Records Administration; p. 17 World Digital Library/U.S. National Archives & Records Administration; p. 18 © CORBIS/Corbis via Getty Images; p. 27 EQRoy/Shutterstock.com; p. 28 Kevin Grant/Shutterstock.com.

Manufactured in the United States of America

CPSIA Compliance Information: Batch #CS18PK: For Further Information contact Rosen Publishing, New York, New York at 1-800-237-9932

CONTENTS

WORDS IN THE GLOSSARY APPEAR IN **BOLD** TYPE THE FIRST TIME THEY ARE USED IN THE TEXT.

TRYING TIMES: THE CIVIL WAR PRESIDENT

When Abraham Lincoln left his home in Illinois to begin the long journey to his **inauguration** as president, he told his neighbors he faced a task "greater than that which rested upon Washington." It was one of the most accurate predictions he ever made. No U.S. president before or after faced a graver crisis or emerged with a greater reputation.

Lincoln took his oath of office on March 4, 1861, assuring southerners they had "no quarrel" with him. But quarrel they did. Southern states had already **seceded** and formed the Confederate States of America, presenting the most severe challenge to national authority in the country's brief history. Then in April, when Confederate forces opened fire on Fort Sumter, South Carolina, Lincoln promptly called for volunteers to defend the Union. The Civil War had begun.

LINCOLN GREW UP ON THE WESTERN FRONTIER. HE LOVED TO READ, AND WAS MOSTLY SELF-EDUCATED. AS A YOUNG MAN, HE PRACTICED LAW, AND EVENTUALLY ENTERED POLITICS.

The Second Battle of Bull Run, pictured here, was fought on August 29th, 1862. The Union Army suffered defeat.

In a special Independence Day message to Congress in 1861, Lincoln called the struggle ahead "a people's contest." He was determined to preserve majority rule, warning that if democracy was defeated in America, it would surely never rise again anywhere in the world.

Words alone did not win victories. Just weeks later, Union forces were crushed at the Battle of Bull Run. A despairing Lincoln realized that the struggle would be long, costly, and bloody, but he steadfastly rejected suggestions that he abandon the war and allow the South to leave the Union in peace.

Union impatience was understandable. The North boasted more men and better technology. The South claimed a brilliant **corps** of generals, including Robert E. Lee, whom Lincoln had tried to recruit to head the Union army. The Union lost again at the Second Battle of Bull Run (August 1862) and the Battle of Fredericksburg (December 1862), and Union forces failed to capture the Confederate capital of Richmond after a long campaign in Virginia.

This image shows President Lincoln signing the Emancipation Proclamation.

In September 1862, General Lee, fearing that southern supplies would eventually run out, invaded Maryland. There, Union forces finally triumphed at the Battle of Antietam, the bloodiest single day in the history of American warfare. Lincoln seized on the victory to issue the **Emancipation** Proclamation. He clearly hoped it would change the course of the war by threatening southern productivity at home—where slaves still worked on farms and plantations while white men fought in the Confederate army.

Lincoln defended his momentous decision by declaring, "We cannot escape history." Although emancipation certainly did change history, it did not immediately change the course of the war. In May 1863, Lee handed the Union one of its worst defeats at the Battle of Chancellorsville.

Meanwhile, many antiwar northerners were demanding peace and openly urging disloyalty to the Union. Lincoln created more **controversy** by allowing military arrests of civilians and prolonged confinement of suspects awaiting trial. The government defended both as attempts to crack down on treason.

In this photograph, Lincoln (circled below) can be seen addressing soldiers and citizens at Gettysburg.

Lincoln also ordered America's first military draft—a highly unpopular, badly conceived system in which wealthy men could buy their way out of service. In July 1863, New York City erupted in riots triggered by the draft. Mobs **lynched** innocent blacks and even burned an orphanage for black children.

Earlier in July, the North won a major victory at the Battle of Gettysburg and captured Vicksburg, Mississippi, the same week. But as 1863 drew to a close, Lincoln probably ranked as the most unpopular president in history.

That November, Lincoln did with words what he had been unable to do with bullets. In a two-minute speech at Gettysburg, he rallied the North to what he called a "new birth of freedom" for America, vowing that government "of the people, by the people, for the people" would not "perish from the earth." It remains the greatest presidential speech ever given.

Lincoln also assumed an increasingly active role as commander in chief. It took him years to find the right generals—he hired and fired them with shocking swiftness in 1861 and 1862—but eventually he found reliable leaders such as Ulysses S. Grant and William T. Sherman.

Below, Frederick Douglass appeals to President Lincoln and his cabinet to allow black soldiers to join Union forces.

In 1864, Lincoln made two major decisions, the importance of which is often overlooked. First, he allowed the presidential election to proceed as scheduled—something unheard of in countries torn by rebellion. In addition, Lincoln decided to run again for the presidency. No president since Andrew Jackson had been reelected to a second term.

The 1864 campaign was one of the ugliest in U.S. history. Lincoln was challenged by one of his former generals, George B. McClellan. McClellan's backers accused Lincoln of supporting intermarriage between blacks and whites, a ploy designed to panic voters.

Until the last few weeks of the campaign, Lincoln believed that he would lose the election. He even asked his own **cabinet** to sign, sight unseen, a pledge to cooperate with the next president. And he secretly plotted with black leader Frederick Douglass to spread news of emancipation in the South to encourage slaves to flee their masters before the next president could overturn the order.

Two months before Election Day, Union forces captured Atlanta, turning the tide of the war. Lincoln went on to defeat McClellan, winning 55 percent of the popular vote and 212 of 233 electoral votes.

John Wilkes Booth shot Lincoln on April 14, 1865. Just days later on April 26, 1865, he himself died of a gunshot wound, inflicted either by a soldier or by himself.

Lincoln's finest moment may have come at his second inaugural on March 4, 1865. He defended the sacrifice of lives that had been necessary to rid America of the evil of slavery and called for an era of "malice toward none" and "charity for all" to "bind up the nation's wounds" and create "lasting peace among ourselves."

The war ended a month later, and Lincoln began working on plans to reconstruct the devastated Union. He even hinted publicly that he would extend the right to vote to those black Americans who had fought to preserve the Union.

One of those who heard Lincoln offer that hope was an actor named John Wilkes Booth. An embittered Confederate sympathizer, Booth, at the urging of several other conspirators, fatally shot Lincoln at Ford's Theatre on April 14, 1865. Nine hours later, Lincoln died in a boarding house across the street.

A man may have died, but a legend was quickly born. Hated by many while he lived, Lincoln was now universally celebrated as a latter-day Moses who had led black Americans to freedom and a beloved **martyr** who had died at the moment of his greatest triumph. More than ever, he seemed to symbolize American opportunity, for as Lincoln had put it, if he could rise from log cabin to White House, "any man's son" could hope to do the same.

THE "GREAT EMANCIPATOR"

Nothing Abraham Lincoln ever did as president aroused so much celebration—and so much anger—as the Emancipation Proclamation. Even now, it remains one of the least understood and most controversial acts in U.S. history.

When it was issued in 1862, many white Americans were outraged, complaining bitterly that it changed the goal of the Civil War from saving the Union to freeing the slaves—a mission many people could not accept. **Ironically**, most complaints about the proclamation today come not from whites but from African Americans, who contend that it accomplished nothing. They argue that the slaves freed themselves by fleeing from plantations on their own.

On September 22, 1862, Lincoln issued his preliminary Emancipation Proclamation, shown here. It stated that as of January 1, 1863, all slaves in rebel states were free.

This illustration shows freed slaves traveling north after the Emancipation Proclamation was officially issued on January 1, 1863.

Lincoln's proclamation was a **moral** landmark. It also was a political stroke of genius that began the long-overdue process of crushing slavery.

To some, it may seem to have offered too little, too late, as it was not issued until the war was nearly two years old and at first it freed slaves only in states over which Lincoln had no control. But Lincoln knew he could not issue his revolutionary document until a majority of white northerners were prepared to accept it and until he was sure it would not drive still-loyal slave states like Maryland into the Confederacy. As for limiting its reach, Lincoln had no legal authority to free slaves in Union states. Instead, the order was based on the commander in chief's power to seize the property of those in rebellion. Unquestionably, the slaves themselves had to accomplish with their feet what Lincoln had begun with his pen.

In this image, Lincoln is shown proclaiming "Freedom for all, both black and white."

Newspapers and politicians the world over attacked Lincoln for daring to free the slaves. More Union soldiers than ever began deserting because of the proclamation. In the months to come, advisors often urged Lincoln to cancel his proclamation, but he steadfastly refused.

Lincoln knew that his order had only begun the work of ending slavery. "The harpoon is in the monster," he said. Now the monster had to be destroyed. To do this, Lincoln encouraged passage of the Thirteenth Amendment of the U.S. Constitution, outlawing slavery everywhere. Despite its passage, if Lincoln were alive today, he would likely be the first to admit that the work of ending slavery still remains unfinished. However, Lincoln truly deserved the title that a grateful America bestowed on him in 1863: "Great Emancipator."

"I LAUGH, BECAUSE I MUST NOT CRY"

Abraham Lincoln often had a look of sadness on his face, but he enjoyed few things more than a good joke. It was an ironic side to the **stoic** leader. A childhood friend once said that even as a young boy, Lincoln was "so funny he could make a cat laugh." Years later, a newspaper called President Lincoln "Chief Joker of the Land." Humor was his way of coping with the stress of a nation at war with itself.

Because he was skinny and not very handsome, Lincoln liked to tell jokes about himself. One favorite was his reply to Stephen Douglas during a debate, after Douglas called him a two-faced liar. "If I had another face," Lincoln said to the audience, "I ask you would I be wearing this one?"

This photograph of Lincoln was taken on August 9, 1963, while the nation he led was at war.

Mary Todd Lincoln, shown here, was First Lady of the United States from 1861 to 1865.

A humorous story Lincoln told was about his first meeting with Mary Todd at a grand ball. Bowing to her, he nervously said that he would like to dance with her "in the worst way." A footsore Mary Lincoln later told a friend, "He certainly did."

As president, Lincoln often used wit with people who annoyed him. When General George B. McClellan kept refusing to engage the enemy in battle, Lincoln sent him a letter saying, "If you don't intend to use the army, won't you lend it to me?" McClellan, upset by Lincoln's barbs and constant requests for reports from the front, turned the tables and sent the president a dispatch asking what to do with "six captured cows." His commander in chief was quick to reply, "Milk them."

Lincoln certainly did not take the war lightly. In fact, the president, who suffered through spells of depression, felt a keen sense of responsibility for the bloodshed. To remain an effective president, he used his humor. "I laugh, because I must not cry," he once said. Today, more than 150 years later, humorous Lincoln stories are still being told. Some really happened. Others are made up. But that wouldn't have bothered Lincoln. When told that his favorite book, Aesop's Fables, was "all lies," he replied, "Mighty darn good lies," and continued reading.

LINCOLN'S OTHER WARTIME TRIUMPHS

Abraham Lincoln won his greatest fame for saving the Union during the Civil War and issuing the Emancipation Proclamation. But in four years in the White House, Lincoln dealt with many other issues, and his handling of them still benefits Americans today. During Lincoln's administration, for example, the nation began the program that led to today's state college system. The Morrill Act of 1862 required that money raised by the sale of public lands granted to each state be used for agricultural education. These land-grant schools later formed the basis for many state university systems still in operation.

IOWA, HOME TO IOWA STATE UNIVERSITY,
WAS THE FIRST STATE IN THE NATION
TO ACCEPT THE PROVISIONS
OF THE MORRILL ACT OF 1862.

Visitors to Washington, D.C., can visit the Lincoln Memorial, built to honor the nation's sixteenth president.

Also in 1862, Congress passed—and Lincoln signed into law—the Homestead Act, which offered Americans up to 160 acres of free land. This law did much to encourage the settlement of the West.

Before Lincoln became president, the United States had only primitive communication and transportation systems. But during his term in office, the country introduced its first free mail delivery service and its first coast-to-coast telegraph operation. Meanwhile, enormous progress was made in linking the nation together by rail.

The fact that the United States could make such progress during a rebellion shows the strength not only of its president, but also of the country itself.

THE FIRST HOMESTEAD IN THE UNITED STATES

GLOSSARY

cabinet: A group of advisers to the US president that is made up of the heads of the executive departments of the government.

controversy: A disagreement that is often heated, public, and lengthy.

corps: A main division of an armed force of the military.

emancipation: Freeing someone from slavery or other legal, social, or political restrictions.

inauguration: The formal admission of someone to a political office.

ironic: Happening in a different way from what is typically expected.

lynched: Killed by hanging for an alleged (unproven) offense without a trial.

martyr: Someone who is killed for their beliefs.

moral: Having to do with understanding the difference between right and wrong behavior.

seceded: Withdrew formally from membership in a federal union, an alliance, or a political or religious organization.

stoic: Calm or unmoved in the face of pain or discomfort.

FOR MORE INFORMATION

BOOKS

Judson, Clara Ingram. *Abraham Lincoln: Friend of the People*. Minneapolis, MN: Young Voyageur, 2016.

Sullivan, George. *Abraham Lincoln: In Their Own Words*. New York: Scholastic Paperbacks, 2001.

WEBSITES

U.S. Presidents / Abraham Lincoln
https://millercenter.org/president/lincoln

Abraham Lincoln
https://www.whitehouse.gov/1600/presidents/abrahamlincoln

Publisher's note to educators and parents: Our editors have carefully reviewed these websites to ensure that they are suitable for students. Many websites change frequently, however, and we cannot guarantee that a site's future contents will continue to meet our high standards of quality and educational value. Be advised that students should be closely supervised whenever they access the Internet.

INDEX